Weight of the Ripened

GINA FERRARA

DOS MADRES

2020

DOS MADRES PRESS INC.
P.O.Box 294, Loveland, Ohio 45140
www.dosmadres.com   editor@dosmadres.com

Dos Madres is dedicated to the belief that the small press is essential to the vitality of contemporary literature as a carrier of the new voice, as well as the older, sometimes forgotten voices of the past. And in an ever more virtual world, to the creation of fine books pleasing to the eye and hand.

Dos Madres is named in honor of Vera Murphy and Libbie Hughes, the "Dos Madres" whose contributions have made this press possible.

Dos Madres Press, Inc. is an Ohio Not For Profit Corporation and a 501 (c) (3) qualified public charity. Contributions are tax deductible.

Executive Editor: Robert J. Murphy

Illustration & Book Design: Elizabeth H. Murphy
www.illusionstudios.net

Typeset in Adobe Garamond Pro & Chopin Script
ISBN 978-1-948017-77-0
Library of Congress Control Number: 2020931966

First Edition

ACKNOWLEDGEMENTS

Grateful acknowledgment is made to the editors of the following journals and anthologies where these poems first appeared:

AIPF di-verse-city Anthology: "One Kind of Genesis"
Autumn Sky Poetry: "Applied"
Dovecote: "Above Whispers at Twenty-One"
Ella Fitzgerald 100 Anthology: "A Reliable Luminosity"
Enchantment of the Ordinary Anthology: "A Small Provenance"
The Kerf: "Living with the River" "Red at First Sight"
Louisiana Literature: "The Batture Defined" "The Light
      Purveyor" "Port City Portrait"
The Lowestoft Chronicle: "Seen on Terpischore"
Third Wednesday: "Her Mauve Palette"
Maple Leaf Rag Anthology: "Nightscape" "Immersion"
      "In and Outside the Confines of a Pink Room"
Miramar: "Lost"
Mockingheart Review: "Most Mornings"
Naugatuck Review: "Seeing Psycho for the First Time"
Ovunque Siamo: "Between Us and Sky" "Rose Rosette"
Panoplyzine: "One Memory I Have of Summer"
The Poets' Billow: "Hunger Moon Habit"
The Swamp: "History"
The Turnip Truck(s): "Affixed"
The UNO MFA Anthology: "That Voice"
Valley Voices: "After Apple Season" and "Another Broken
      Curfew"
Xavier Review: "Without Any Kind of Rhetoric"

Gratitude

I express much thanks and gratitude to family, friends, poets, colleagues, and collaborators, and always, special thanks to my husband, Jonathan Kline, for all of our days and years together.

Table of Contents

I. Clustered

II. From Vines

III. *In Groves*

IV. *Rampant*

I
Clustered

Weight of the Ripened

Gravity would not allow my father's favorite fruit
to dangle from a branch or limb, to be plucked
or picked, the absurd weight,
a matter, all matter extended from root and vine,
prevented any theft or pocketing of the obvious
when he stopped by roadsides,
at pick up trucks, flatbeds filled with nearly a pyramid
to lift then thump the striated skin
a range from chartreuse to deep jade,
the weight carried beneath his arm
shared a tantruming toddler's size.
There was no talk of history or origin.
Each time he took his knife with the vast blade,
that held a glint with a single purpose,
inserting only the tip, gripping the handle
to delve the blade deeper—
a momentary disappearance and lodging
before halves opened in longevity
each side separated with the scope
of a heart or robust hemisphere,
red fruit enmeshed with the random
accumulation of black seeds.

Explaining the Superlative

The closest we will ever come
where I endeavor
and you will fathom
how a slivered moon
and the reliable light of Venus
is one definition of dappled throughout a sequel
or recurrence each time,
the staid shadows unstirred in this stillness
define what it is to emulate after dark.

Blossoms the length of millimeters
appear as small lacerations
without harm or a sun to illuminate
to be embellished by a golden light
intensifying beneath the constellated
to enter our house heavier than a phantom
with an intense sweetness
and saturation that vanishes by dawn.

One Memory I Have of Summer

The fence obscured by honeysuckle
with numberless trumpets heralding
droplets, miniscule beads of nectar.

A jet scrapes the sky, scratches reality,
the white line straight without intersection
leaves only part of a cross traveling one way
in an uninterrupted soliloquy further south.

Every day lily opens without secret,
the mottled and the solid
mouth silent arias, unabashed and blooming.

The bird house replicates our own
wood painted in moon beam, evergreen shutters,
and silver dollar sized apertures constricted in refusals,
too narrow for even the smallest sparrow to enter.

Judy's Doll Ginny

Not long after Plath's suicide
and the wall being erected,

each upright inch made me scream
as Ginny stood taller than any yardstick.

My sister, guiding, to become obscured by a toy,
her clunky plaything approaching

dangerous as atomic capability
a doll, statuesque, with a state-run gait,

clunky propaganda, superior, super imposed,
the formidable distance of then and before.

She moved down the corridor's length,
in strappy patent leather shoes,

as if stepping over decomposition and aftermath,
two decades beyond Stutthoff, Treblinka,

bones from Auschwitz, and Dachau
fallen ashes absorbed where tulips

and hyacinths clustered, abloom, somewhere
the missiles pointed, ready for instantaneous launch.

Dense, impenetrable, onyx lashes covered
plexiglass eyes brighter than azure,

framed by flaxen, straight bangs,
slightly smocked in her pinafore red dress.

Unable to speak from my doorway
I watched Ginny emerge life-sized

as one type of threat, mine,
on warm days during those cold years.

Another Broken Curfew

Since I left the intricacy
of what had been wrought

in the corner, the sheer gauze,
a gossamer, newly formed,

fly away filaments, a sheen of uncertainty,
headlights illuminating,

illuminating my mother spectral and epic
in the doorway, she stood barefoot.

A pain came with my arrival—
maybe she felt the first jolt,

uncanny, nearly electric,
the noise almost levitating her

one hour before the sky became unstuck;
my mother heard the engine

each cylinder annunciating
then backfiring, the audacity,

the wheezing, the rough idle
on the verge of undulating,

the boy who departed
with only the two syllables of his name.

Where the Reeds Were Higher

We crossed the wide planked bridge
where the reeds were higher
I spotted your father's navy sedan
parked with its tidy interior and whitewalls

I started to wave then stopped

you were examining the bearded irises
mottled purple and white

some scant yellow
close to the water
the woman wasn't your mother

his hands held her head
at the nape
caressing her crown
platinum locks slipping
cascading between and over his fingers

your father had no beard
his face smooth and shaven
brushed with scented talc
earlier that morning I suspected
you did not

I pointed to a papery white egret taking flight
legs looking like they'd snap
as your father turned the key and drove
along the road that curved
snake-like away from city limits

Most Mornings

I watched my mother's continuity,
how far it could extend,
that single minded purpose
never spliced or severed
from wherever she stood to the horizon,
the unequivocal seam she sought spanning
the distance to reach without a complaint
or deviation when she left for work
in navy, black or gray, her day long
attire for the living or the dead,
reconciling the inevitable
and leaving me to sleep,
to face the cool stucco wall,
painted the color of a fractured sunrise.

I Dream Of

Dusk, rubbing my grandmother's heels,
nearly creating a magical collision of air,
with hot and cold evergreen
ointment permeating as one wish
granted, where the skin curves,
chapped and chaffed
from the relentless realities
of touching the ground.

In that tarnished brass bottle,
the plush pillows, ovals and octagons, tassled,
pressed in velvets, brocades
of burgundies and purples,
Nana says Jeannie seems trapped
by wishes and commands,
the confines of being corked and capped,
a suspect in her pink harem pants.

*O*de to the Indigenous

After the city slipped and became a wound
without a tourniquet, bleeding old
with the new no one knew,
the treasures like the indigenous,
where the crepe myrtles grew
from south to north, the magenta, lavender,
pink and white in tandem
and clustered looking bleach barked, barely
bending towards the lake…summer,
the scent of brine and the bridge lights
illuminated, smaller than pin pricks in shades of amber
for twenty five miles before the horizon,
the point with the darkened light house,
splashy staccatos—jagged rocks breaking waves
the big tree in the park, just beyond the labyrinth,
the bend in the distance where we sat watching
vessels pass with faded letters and foreign flags,
tankers carrying barrels and grain flanked by tugboats,
how the cicadas signaled the start of imminent Augusts
    and Septembers
without being seen from the apexes of oaks.

Bird of Paradise

Dormancy breaks, like an eruption,
such rupture comes without a warning or hiss.
On this still earth the clash of orange
and dark purple avowed
in conjugal descent, the purple
emulates, elongated and explanatory.
A petal projects, in tufts and petulant tongue
with last words far beyond the vernacular.
From reeds with undulating leaves, edges serrate,
incorrigible color rises without ever taking flight.

Without Any Kind of Rhetoric

The difficulties of hearing those words,
stating every time you planned to cut my hair,
that grew the length of an unnamed river,
without a basin, vital from scalp to end,
the scissors you'd use, I knew them,
saw them idle and flat in the drawer,
the heavy black ones, the relics
with their legacy of clipping the tethered.

Your threat to rid me of ringlets, tangled origins,
and the big bang of strands
knotted against my neck,
the castaways of random ribbons
satin, soft yarn, grosgrain, untied,
and unruly locks, years spanning
from here to there, falling like severed longitudes
to cover the earth.

Immersion

Sunlight cannot penetrate tupelos and cypresses,
the indigenous canopies
or crape myrtle ones…the oaks are connected
interlocked in collusion wound with resurrection fern.
This is the unabashed to walk through
over the uprisings of mushrooms with their death caps
and tilted parasols, no chanterelles, or pleasing pinkish reds
to tumble without a sound into the pail.
You are always on the verge of slipping further,
especially without echelons or stratum in this landscape.
Something decomposes,
loses its sinew and form,
its fur, its skin, muscle and mass,
a moment of recognition and return
smelling like the hour after.

In and Outside the Confines of a Pink Room

Imagined endings,
the tragedies became larger,
elephantine and ambling,
pink stucco walls, dark cameos, tumultuous sunsets,
the coolness of plaster with traceable fissures
on summer nights, after equinox,
the defiant heat settling, not rising,
an ache for October's arrival
a search for more than one word,
a ceiling, an attic, a rafter,
a roof always impeding the stars,
windows nailed shut to ward off intruders
while allowing jasmine
and honeysuckle the little yellow trumpets
their silent sweetness to seep and saturate
not on the moors or sprawling meadows.
Each night we turned the lock,
turned it equatorially until the bolt clicked
in our city, filled with the certainty of sinking.

Applied

It is dark…you are unable to see
the cloudy mirror
a troubled lagoon makes it worse.
The lipstick unsteadily applied
in shakes and quivers, smears,
not a description or a noun,
no, this is a verb, all movement
that bleeds tropical,
a pride of Barbados,
a hand-sized hibiscus
across your lips
marking them as reckless
to give kisses, to retort or purse.
You could use some parchment,
a tissue, to blot the hemorrhage,
this glide of paraben and balm
beyond glib that comes from a tube
with its counterclockwise twist
sharing the motion of the next storm.

II

From Vines

More than One Synonym
(For Moose Jackson)

We are driving to see the crevasse,
of French origin, spoken in romantic
tongues, the place of opening,
the scissure appearing like a wound,
a sudden gash that never scars
because in any given lifetime,
it will not heal, mass, clot or coalesce.
Deep and deeper to something beyond superlative,
a great cleft widens, a noticeable inflection.
The wayward oaks meant to be counted
along the road, nearly genuflecting,
before invisible gods,
limbs bent, raised almost in worship,
giving praise to the imagined,
trunks upright or rising, rising,
at impossible angles and unspoken parallels.
Beneath the canopy, north and southbound,
moss grazes, drapes in descent
every year of a languid century.

assia

The proliferation will make you swallow
intentions, uncontrollable and punctuated.
You will interrogate the falsely pious,
anyone who tries to suppress by uprooting
and will not applaud the unabashed
cascading always in November
closer to goldenrod then saffron.
In silent avalanches, the unadulterated
proclaims itself through pure color.
The planter remains unknown,
anonymous, a previous occupant
with a shovel that struck dirt along the fence,
giving terrain to your only horizon, duplicated
somewhere south of a place never visited,
brought today by the bend and spray in descent,
untamed flowers you hesitate to name or prune—
every petal steeped with the promise of something better
as your fingers pull apart braided trilogies of branches.

History

Maybe it was the Spitfire or Triumph,
the barely yellow or white car, something imported—
bucket seats, with a shift and loaf-sized hump between driver
and passenger, bar in place, the heavy vinyl affixed,
protecting my mother's hair, chiffon scarf forgotten,
top up, blocking glimpses of Orion and the dog star,
or earlier in their history, another car,
the Chevy with red seats and no power steering,
sturdier than a tank, a testimony to chrome.
Did it matter? That humid night,
a corona, an unprecedented halo
surrounding the moon when my parents
traveled east of Chef Menteur, past the Rigolets
and the lighthouse, ninety miles to hear Ray Charles.

Seeing Psycho for the First Time

Two months until the due date,
on a Saturday night
in the theater, the downtown Joy,
epic curtains tufted and separated,
my mother's back presses
against a silent crush of velvet.
She feels a meager fist curl,
the bony protuberance of an elbow or knee
pushes with persistence on her lowest rib.
To find a place of comfort,
she positions and repositions
thinking the screen is too close.
The woman in the seat ahead
has a high bee hive.
A waft of melted butter drifts in tandem
with the monosyllabic pops of each kernel
quickening from the marbled mezzanine
where my father waits in line
for caramels and a cola to share
during the glossiness of each celluloid scene,
film and photograph in full confluence
from the shower head's shine and polished luster,
thin streams of bent water,
evidence vanishing via a vortex
beneath Janet Leigh's stare,
wider than any question,
the torn shower curtain and hooks
move like small bells of warning
as I stir symbiotic and unborn.

Without a Crash

Tender promise by November's light
it was a time for balance while moving
pushing pedals to create a cycle,
a momentum to foster the chains and wheels
the bouncy rubber with treads and spokes,
chrome glinting to suggest a fractured solidity—
a smashed star hurled with force from above,
that silvery radiation, the suggested stellar
aligned with trajectory,
the oaks stoic, roots buckling in small eruptions,
acorns dropping the size of bullets from the canopy
I dodged the sing song notion of the sky falling,
my sister's laughter at my wobbling and the small
protuberant whiteness of my own knuckles
as I gripped, staring ahead, lured by the distance
and the lilting hallelujahs I wanted to hear.

Port City Portrait

A day's measure the length of raw sugar cane
found in the sizable shadows cast by ships
with dissipating and newly christened names
The SS Fatima, The Aolian Vision, The Osaka
Express, The Sidsel Knudsen, on France Road,
Jackson Avenue, Nashville, Piety,
Harmony, Napoleon, Jourdan, or Tchoupitoulas
recited aloud, a syncopation, upriver, downriver,
the wharves where my grandfather worked—
with thick black soles, suede shoes, reliable
and rounded at the toes, laces tied taut,
his hair, unruly as any great river, combed,
slicked down into submission, a stevedore's
cadence marked by a quick current,
the language of levels, rising and falling,
vessels far beyond the vernacular, tugs
accompanying tankers in tandem,
measurements of gross weights, volumes,
arrivals, departures, carrying the prohibited
with the legitimate…winesaps, papayas,
persimmons, handfuls of Brazilian nuts,
and unripe mangos—removed
from the wrinkled brown bag
each dusk, then placed like offerings
to thank or sway the gods.

he Turtle

We leave before the late news
to get cigarettes and milk.
Crossing to walk on the levee,
we spot a turtle stuck as a Pontiac
with an oil leak in the middle of the road.
Cars could come from either direction.
The hissing turtle is not pleased
when we scoop and run with it,
a ticking bomb, away from
manicured lawns with rotary daisies,
white and fantastical in moonlight.
The turtle, round as a green grape in Eden,
leaves the sloping banks, bobs,
follows the current, then disappears
into unfathomable depths
of russet water named for a zealot saint.

$\mathcal{S}$een on Terpsichore

I have lost count of the blooms
entwined, cascading
down the steep pitch,
two spinster dormers, agape, missing panes,
a slow swallow more golden
than what slips from the shell,
the sphere floating and raw,
no accident and full intention approaching
the cusp of a clinging peach
something civilized
served in a parfait glass
observed in odd syllables
with brush and ink
only the written and wrought
hide the roof of its slates,
black diagonals, asphalt diamonds
on Terpsichore untouched by the rain.

Her Mauve Palette

From pink camellia frost to sun splendid plum,
amaranth lotuses afloat in placidity
those preferential shades—
waxy solids never garish or patriotic red
coral remained relegated
to deep water reefs.
My mother didn't line her lips
to form the perfect bow
or prevent color from bleeding
with sudden smiles or grimaces.
The impact of her mauve palette,
in the uppermost vanity drawer
each tube upright, encased,
measured longer than a rifle's bullets
ready for application and wear always
with the smallest counterclockwise twist.

Hunger Moon Habit

Our clandestine mother daughter ride
the steady shafts of headlights,
closer than moonbeams,
of oncoming traffic and parallel white lines,

the ascent and swift descent
when you said it was a hunger moon,
mother, a hunger moon
that night of my birth,
you labored and pushed me through,
the twisted cord of yourself,
cut for me to breathe
to catch the world
with my first breath.

Every year we celebrated my arrival
the glittery cards with pastel sentiments,
a special promise in prismatic light.
I wanted to savor the hard candy,
the solid lozenge, that speckled euphoria,
and layers of sweet butter cream that arrived
with tiny flames on candles always counted
knowing each year your habit
came with the rush of a hundred hooves.

Circa '79

Green gold succotash
simmered, grease popped always
cacophonous from the heaviest black skillet.
Don't ask what kind of South, the light
blinding from a bulb without a shade
full of happenstance halos and actual glare,
illumination in every language, that kind of fluency
all one hundred watts, beyond bright
the superlative, stark white, revealing tiny cuticles,
parallel capillaries, intentions,
and tragic flaws, shining,
breaking the dark of a quiet intersection
when hating pleats came with hating plaid.
Most mothers would have shot him
any suitor in his leisure suit,
the blue one, faded sky, lighter than cerulean
had he tried to slip through the narrow opening
in those houses where windows were nailed,
punctuated by omegas
to barely raised levels of no entries or escapes.

A Small Provenance

After the hurricane, it came on a pallet
the warmest measure of good will
from a few seasons past,
missing one abalone
and mother of pearl button,
cast aside by a Parisian
needing another echelon of style
for crossing nine bridges, throwing tulips
petal after petal afloat in the Seine,
a scene within a scene.
This coat still has swing, moving
from noun to verb to noun with each stride
taken along pavements and banquettes
flaring around my knees, the bottom hem
a soundless bell, black
as any woolen night
minus the accoutrement of stars.

The Tuesday After

The cream took three attempts
before the consistency was right.

I added the milk, cornstarch, thin cascades
of streaming sugar, beaten eggs
and small caps full of vanilla

over a blue-indigo tooth-sized flame while stirring
the spoon scraping the bottom like a dirge,

constantly, dissolving lumps. Eventually,
the cream solidified fluent to flawless,
with a type of mass smooth enough to spread

between two square layers
of your cake I garnished

with chopped dark chocolate,
pieces of pecans and halved maraschinos

when you arrived the Tuesday after
your birthday.

III
In Groves

Homage to a Tangerine in Winter

Taken from a bowl
that once occupied a still life
vacillating from ochre to orange
during this sun absent week,
a tangerine with exotic origins
that drip citrus in three
syllables and soft consonants
skin taut at apex,
imagine a slant rhyme
never mentioned in Eden
the antonym escapes
as fingers pull downward
in deconstruction,
the essence of this and yes
before pulp and separable segments
tendrils of rind curl
from small remnants of stem,
more tangible than anything defined.

Jagged Red Pieces

After you left, one obsession
was easier than the other,
the scent of lilies by the small footbridge
arched high, an expression of surprise over water,
the departure from paths of ampersands
to contiguous stretches and distances
between points,
the hours spent trying to repair
the broken plate,
all the shards lined
in succession like days of the week:
jagged red pieces
the size of runes
cupped then placed on the table
when the moon was my inspiration.

The Light Purveyor

Among the things she kept
on Deer Island or the Head of the Passes,
the Point of Pontchartrain, or on the cusp
of that last impetus of river
flowing into the gulf,
her log written in onyx ink, the tin of buttons
mother of pearl, coins, scraps of poplin
hearty clasps, and eye hooks.
Her vertical existence
both stoic and statuesque
wasn't comfortable on stately avenues
or marbled atriums, her home
a pillar, symbolic and synonymous,
a beacon surrounded
by schools of fish,
seaweed cursively adrift, and brine
touching the tight horizon.
A swirl of steps made of cypress,
to begin the day, to start the night.
Shared with the pelicans and seagulls,
the vantage point, what was seen
and what could be spotted
surrounded by the symmetry
of four cornered panes at apex.
The kerosene, uncapped,
poured like persuasion,
a ready illuminant
drenching the dry wick.

Nightscape

Here I am seeing what can't be dispelled,
this large truth to the rumor with you
the darkest blue ever imagined
it could almost pass for amphibious skin—
nocturnal, a sustainable stain of memory
before the tower appears
that will cast filigree shadows—
a sky that cannot be owned
or burdened by possession
then marked by a trite apostrophe—
its stars nearly superimposed
and dangling with golden points
like harmless little stalactites
too high to grasp.
Layers upon layers—
the immediacy of inextinguishable light
beams, coronas, unbroken rings
stipple the river like single notions
and discarded etceteras.

After Apple Season

(February 11, 1963, Plath's suicide)

it wasn't a silken sari,
from yards of saffron
flattened that night,
to soften the surface—loops worn
the towel once Venetian blue…
rolled with an anaconda's thickness,
premeditated and placed beneath the door sill,
the cloth barrier isolating
what would remain and be taken…
enough to muffle and suppress
where did she leave the unperforated,
the week old wax and stamp,
black shoes without mates,
hidden like small fugitives under the bed
notes for the mandolin,
ecru linens in locked luggage…
the children slept,
one had strep,
the other teething, enamel,
emerging from feverish gums,
bread and milk after daybreak
to quell the sleep broken
shard sharp hunger…
another icicle would not melt
over a two burner stove,
the infernal side by side,
blue grooved flames,
the inside of the oven

a mammoth cave,
a starless galaxy…
one final glance out the window
to see the solitary tree, leafless,
naked, blanched and deciduous,
decisively ready
to lacerate the thinnest light
of moon.

December Homecoming

Segueing to scorched peach, in desperation
the sun clung, the shortest day of the year,

darker at the core as I pulled cuticles
real and imagined when we rode in the ambulance provided,

fulfilling one of your remaining wishes, the last, to be home,
no sirens or speedy arrivals or dispatches of despair

emergencies behind us, the obvious absence ahead.
I held the last bouquet I brought you, in tissue

less than a dozen, swaddled, open blossoms,
turning plaintive in shades meant to preempt pain.

We set up your bed next to the tree, laced with white lights
decorated with angels celebrating the nascent and the imminent,

all of them identical, nearly flaxen, shimmering opalescent
without hesitation weighted with glittery specks on wings,

thin wire halos, gold shrouds grazing ankles,
hands clasped, each one hanging by a hook.

Beyond Retraction

There was no playground that day
No monkey bars and children
Fingers, fists around bars
Twisting alternatives
Of what came before and after
Or slides offering unstoppable descents
With collisions and sudden catastrophes
Not then when you told me
In italicized terms
It was where you needed to go
The swings you imagined
In the shape of crescents
With longitudinal chains
Back and forth you saw yourself
Pushing me toward twilight
That held glimmers of Venus
And passing chevrons of flocks
Though thousands of days had passed
Since you put each end together
To tie the laces of my shoes

Above Whispers at Twenty-One

Jim tried to kiss you at midnight
The cowbell shook small explosions to celebrate
You were the stark obvious zebra
In a room this is how the year started
Cornered you heard confessions
The girl he brought says she was raped

When? A long time ago she was raped
The minutes barely collected since midnight
The room a whirl for any confessions
Jamaican rum, lime wedges, and tequila to celebrate
This is not how you wanted to start
A story unfolding, brazen, bold as a zebra

Nothing will domesticate a zebra
You struggled to hear details of the rape
Her voice wouldn't stop after it started
The drawl, adrift, then drowning before midnight
The novelty of the year celebrated
Jim kissed you minutes after without a confession

And what of your own confessions
You wanted to run unseen in tall grass with the zebras
On a silent plain without celebrations
Narrative falling as dark stains on white, she was raped
It was the first hour after midnight
And hard to delineate where the stripes ever started

A singular wish to finish fast after the start
Was it Jim no admission or confession
A millennium would not arrive after this midnight
Elusive, patterns, black and white wild zebras
Slanted stripes, pluralized and singular rape
Tonight, nothing to be celebrated

Auld Lang Syne segues every year celebrated
The possibility and prospects, the synonymous start
Jim's date above whispers confided she was raped
You listened to her only confession
Jim said your stripes reminded him of zebras
Running from him and the distance of midnight

Spoken tonight, narrow to wide confessions
The harem, the herd, black and white zebras
Galloping untamed, hooves hitting the terrain at midnight

Unequivocally Passing

After the letters having no stamps had been written
and years of uncelebrated birthdays,
along with a scent of brine,
the horizons appeared,
each marked by burnt orange, inextinguishable,
rageful nearly,
darker purples sharing discolorations
of traumatized skin,
though ahead and forefront
suggesting what was yet to begin,
they reminded you of all that you outlived
trains traveling unequivocally
bearing zebra striped inflated letters
a noticeable camouflage—
tags on almost every boxcar
linked in succession
the dramatic jump
with a hoist then a heave
the ultimate departures
when descriptions came with unwanted synonyms.

In the Time of Japanese Magnolias

Another shooting, the eighteenth
this year just before spring.
The carnage is unbearable
as unstoppable torch petals swell.
In silence, the blooms are scattered
across the expanse of dry grass,
uprisings of clovers along the edges.

One fits in your hand with the shared
size of a small bird, a rescued sparrow,
that fell from the apex
a held contradiction of weightlessness
nearly filling the space of a grasp,
and an idea that floating
lotus like is possible
if placed on the surface
of water.

Seasonal and Beyond

It's January, days after the freeze killed,
killed each tropical, the litany of my garden,
lavender lantana, the night blooming jasmine,
the birds of paradise, the irises and ginger lilies,
even the evergreens lack verdant depth.

Jonathan says I can't live north
in the winter when everything
looks like this—
only worse and more sparse,
poised and still enough to injure.

I have a hard time with loss even reading
about the sage grouse habitat
no longer an oasis and the real threat
of things being irreversible,
the damage too deep,
seeping through the tissues beyond scarring,
when the resurrection fern needs more than rain.

That Voice *(For Nason Smith)*

I told you once about country music,
the way it reminded me of a one-eyed cat
and sizable rust spots on a metal pail,

busted carburetors leaking oily pools filled
with happenstance iridescence, how most of it
made me want to scream, to self-annihilate

to just surrender when it was time for a fight,
the tales of loving til the day after forever
from the depths of a cell or distillation measured in years.

No glee or joy came from telling you
that your idol was dead, your legend,
Merle, whose own mamma said

he was, as a child, incorrigible,
capable of stretching elastic to eternity,
whose voice you heard with or without revolutions

holding the exact cadence and conditions
of half-patched threadbare brothers and the father
you wouldn't bring yourself to bury.

A Reliable Luminosity

I want to listen to Ella Fitzgerald today.
New year is near and the world continues
with its realities….the debates rage,
a gun jams, too many go off,
too many mood and actual triggers
that put us in the wrong state,
too many denials, too few
conversations that lead to somewhere.
I want to listen to Ella Fitzgerald today
and imagine all the women in black dresses,
the kind my mother wore, crepe or velveteen
lined in satin, a *peau de soie* with a singular
strand of pearls that holds a reliable luminosity.
The men know the meaning of special occasions.
Along with keys and four cornered cuff links,
they have chrome
and stainless steel lighters…they remembered
to buy flints and fluid on the way home.
The pressed table linens come to chevrons,
strategic diagonal points,
that graze the knees or shins as a given and only a given.
Cocktail shakers make ice collide in hard consonants,
with bitters and bourbon almost in unison;
mostly everyone is drinking scotch,
on the cusp of finishing the first round.
The candles flicker but not with the same
brightness or virtuosity of Ella
whose notes and improvised syllables
elicit applause during and after every song.

Without Owls

No hoots or screeches,
no horned, snowy, ashy faced,
northern tawny, cinnamon, golden masked,
vericulated, Tasmanian
pharaoh eagle, white throated,
long tufted, cloud forest,
bare-shanked, bearded,
flammulated, black capped,
whiskered or common barn,
none of the trees nest owls.
They do not perch in the boughs
near the trunks' mysterious hollows.
They do not roost in the eaves
just beneath the highest point of apex.
They do not fly above the roof
by a moon now hours beyond risen.
They do not swoop silent field mice
scurrying quick and syllabic in a moment.
The night is owl-void, owl-otherwhere,
owl-uninhabited, owl-desolate,
owl-absent, missing
any sense of omniscience.

espire

Fragile gardenia.
Any scent of paradise is lost.
Now the leaves are black,
marked with pocks in patterns
that are the antithesis of constellations,
closer to cancerous
as dreaded spots on lungs.

These are real just like the pebble sized
mark that appeared on the x-ray.
Blind-sided. The ripples were made
for the inanimate to waver.

You gave up cigarettes forever,
the habitual inhaling and exhaling
gray white smoke in solitary letters
hanging ampersands and lurid rings,
the last unfiltered pack
crumpled into submission
so that your lungs might expand
to the size of what happens next.

IV

Rampant

Affixed

Enough to form filigree Eiffel Towers to surround
a triptych of gemstones and treasured tenses of time,
one strand, one antenna twitches with potential to
pass
through the needle's unwavering eye,
when what's spun becomes a small genesis.

The insect moves without revolution
leaving orbits to planets, momentum to avalanches,
positions then repositions, to ascend and descend,
as plotted points on a graph marking capability and
decline.

Against the thin wire mesh
head, thorax, legs and idle wings
measure the size of a matriarchal brooch,
a coveted heirloom glinting in amber
with a moonstone underside.

Red At First Sight

No onion, no skin,
the redness makes me stop.
I catch my breath, gasping
at the sight of what appears,
absent of contact with serrated edges—
the blur becomes actualized and still.
My fingers cease and lift momentarily
from the letters of an orderly alphabet
when the cardinal arrives
without precursors or segues,
fully masked singing three quick notes
missives for any civilization
in that narrow space
between the balusters.

*R*ose *Rosette*

Needing more than to prune
and uproot, it was time, the hour
to burn, to douse flammable fragments
in one contiguous stream,
and follow with a strike not meant for extinguishing
each branch, the smaller canes
exaggerated with thorns and scarlet bristles
irate extremities at the tips in kerosene
to destroy the mites, an unseen cavalry
that came with the wind from any direction
causing the whites, always hesitant
to internalize before stopping,
quelling each rose to nothing more than memory,
the dark reds and pinks at one time
I brought you bound by nothing
more than wet tissue.

One Kind of Genesis

Muddy baubles,
bulb after bulb,
a broken strand that never held
mysteries or glimmer,
my mother's vision
became a madness
from here to the horizon:
the narcissi,
the tulips,
Scheherazades
allegrettos,
arabesques,
and cathedral windows
hording a flame,
even ones spotted
like great sitting leopards
ready to leap,
to turn predatory,
her variations of lilies
with syllables and potential
tumbled from the trowel's tongue
into an overly pliant earth
ready to root and sprout

The Angel Fish

A dilated eye, a cameo, a notion,
a button, a round gun metal dollar
moving without stealth
a full snow moon
silvery striated circumference
banished from all variations of heaven
above jade green gravel
through stone pagodas
and beneath bunches of unripe bananas
devouring nearly an alphabet of small guppies
before swallowing the solitary
liquid laser light of tetras,
we were duped by your name.

The Batture Defined

With no thought of mountains
or the madness of mohair or cashmere,
I'll take you with a promise
to the batture, a bending place,
a sinewy earth, a lauded bed,
of permanence, woven with willowy words
sweet alliterative, aloud, and alluvial
the indigenous intricacies of admissions
and verses, irises, steeped darker than lavender,
flecked yellow before us
each emblazoned with stars
of a single dimension, indolent flames
of flattened tongues on the city's edge.

Between Us and the Sky

One canopy of cloth

named in three syllables,

sometimes ruffled, vowels and double

consonants, hands

gripping close to the curve

the inquisitive, at the pole's end,

the bamboo hook, supple stitched leather,

the mahogany handle, the eternally rhetorical

opening to an enviable span,

nearly wider than anything avian.

Mists and squalls fall in the moment

the predicted and the unexpected,

canvases stretched taut, blacks, navys,

bladder sized peonies proliferating an occasional red,

ribs extended, a tenacious opacity,

a history of sheltering beneath cloudbursts,

segues, separations, schisms

and a steadfast sun.

Living with the River

To flood, to recede
to fill each epoch, the river
wants what it wants, to meet the gulf
by cumulative, immeasurable seconds, inflicted,
infected, reluctant to heal
from a wound, a deeply given gash.
By sun and moonlight
the river is many shades
of dried blood, passing the marshes,
the mangroves, the empty estuaries,
and the barrier islands becoming less
pluralized, once lined like blades
ready to scale fish, peel citrus, and sheer cyclones.
The river deliberates and wants to shift,
to form its own opinion, to renege
on its unmade promise, a matter of course,
absent of guidance, with a telepathic current
to find and flow by fate in just the right way.

$\mathcal{L}$ost

Beyond explanation
always searching, the constant rummage
for the eyeglasses, the wallet,
the shoes, only one of them,
the aced test, the acid test, the failed
test, the prescription, the trust, the book
of sonnets, the logic, the phone number,
the bill, the earring, the sock, the slipper,
the desire, the pearls, the story, the stamps,
the recipe, the pen, the lipstick, the number,
the note, the map, the corkscrew, the clippers,
the ticket, the key, the glove, the breath mints,
the nouns of our lives soon become invisible,
unseen as the axis tilting the world.

Impossible Pairings

You appeared barefoot at my door.
I noticed the dirt on your toes
and purposeful heels
as if you had been following
the dusty paths of Galilee,
but these were not biblical times
for you came to the house
in search of shoes
which I piled into an unused playpen.
All of the shoes were black, yet
none of them matched,
as you hopelessly paired
thong with moccasin sandal with boot.
I kept the essential knowledge
of having buried all of the mates in the backyard,
beneath the lure of the secretive fig tree
as I watched you walk
away from the house
into the direction of nameless clouds,
waiting, to welcome you in the distance.

Green Dress Escapade

A hard hazard, trapped in the dress
I cannot exit, the zipper jammed
as any window nailed shut
with the finality of a crucifixion
in an infernal building once condemned
where the act of arson begins soon
surrounded by many dialects of flaming tongues
and without a chair to hurl, stuck
my arms too short, fingers unable to pinch or grasp
the shiny tab, silver, ever elusive with a lift and tug,
to travel the entire length of a toothy longitude
wanting to release the creasing emerald silken sea
into the necessity of opposites.

Morning Glory

From the jalousies, in perfect view
purple, the regality of it
comes with its own glory,
blooming just after sunrise
never as dark as last night's sky,
opening petal for petal
as a yes, a deep affirmation
in the thickest drape
covering the chain link
and wooden fences
with the potential
that each ensuing hour holds.

Before Torpor

In search of the alliterative
Neruda's nectar, from lantana
to red bottle brush filaments,
the succulent lull and allure,
somewhere there is foam, frothing,
lacing aquamarine and deep water azure,
the taste and quick sting of salt,
the tepid embrace near the ankles,
a phantom brush of seaweed,
and further, the cool inexplicable pockets,
but not here, the cursive patterns,
created by a pair of hummingbirds
in tandem then synchronized
an invisible alphabetic pattern
the same fingers of a different hand
miles from any ocean
that beckons.

About the Author

GINA FERRARA lives in New Orleans and teaches English and writing at Delgado Community College where she is an associate professor. Her poetry collections include: *The Size of Sparrows* (Finishing Line Press 2006) *Ethereal Avalanche* (Trembling Pillow Press 2009) *Amber Porch Light* (CW Books 2013), *Carville: Amid Moss and Resurrection Fern* (FLP 2014) and *Fitting the Sixth Finger: Poems Inspired by the Paintings of Marc Chagall* published by Aldrich Press in 2017. Her work has appeared in *Callaloo, The Tar River Review, The Poetry Ireland Review* and others. She is an Elizabeth George Foundation grant recipient, and she curates The Poetry Buffet, a monthly reading series held The Latter Branch of the New Orleans Public Library.

For the full Dos Madres Press catalog:
www.dosmadres.com